COPING WITH
CYBERBULLYING

Jeff Mapua

New York

Published in 2018 by The Rosen Publishing Group, Inc.
29 East 21st Street, New York, NY 10010

First Edition

Library of Congress Cataloging-in-Publication Data

Names: Mapua, Jeff, author.
Title: Coping with cyberbullying / Jeff Mapua.
Description: First Edition. | New York, New York: Rosen Publishing, 2018. | Series: Coping | Audience: Grades 9–12. | Includes bibliographical references and index.
Identifiers: LCCN 2016059973 | ISBN 9781508173939 (library bound)
Subjects: LCSH: Cyberbullying—Juvenile literature. | Cyberbullying—Prevention—Juvenile literature.
Classification: LCC HV6773.15.C92 M337 2018 | DDC 302.34/302854678—dc23
LC record available at https://lccn.loc.gov/2016059973

Manufactured in the United States of America

CONTENTS

INTRODUCTION

Cell phones, tablets, laptops, wearable devices, and other electronics are all around us nowadays. People can connect with one another at a moment's notice, any time of the day or night. A new generation is growing up having never known a life before the internet. Digital lives and reputations are taken seriously, as seriously as "IRL" (in real life). However, along with the enhanced ability to communicate online come the negative aspects of social life and the ugly side of human behavior.

Many are familiar with bullying in the traditional sense. A bully at school, for example, will tease or threaten someone they see as weak or defenseless. The threats can intensify and even lead to physical violence. Though a serious concern in the days before everyone lived online, bullies could only torment those physically in their presence. Cyberbullying, on the other hand, can happen any hour of the day, on any day of the week, regardless of whether someone is at school, at home, or anywhere. It takes place over the Internet, via cell phones, smartphones, computers, tablets, and other devices.

Cyberbullies can use popular social media sites, text messaging, online chats, and any number of websites as tools of harassment. They are the culprits behind mean texts, threatening emails, and hurtful rumors that circulate via social media. Other forms of harassment include sharing embarrassing photos or videos online using one of the many image-sharing applications teens use in their daily lives. There have also been cases where cyberbullies create fake profiles and personas online with the sole intention of bullying their victims.

Because it is easy to hide one's true identity online, vicious posts can be made anonymously. This anonymity makes it difficult to find out who is responsible for a threatening or embarrassing post. Worse still, a post, message, image, or video online can reach a wide audience extremely quickly. Distributing content over the Internet is a simple click away, and a victim can see a rumor spread like wildfire. As many have had to learn the hard way, taking down a message online is extremely difficult once it has been posted.

Not all cyberbullies restrict their abusive behavior to the online world. Cyberbullying is associated with bullying in person, and vice versa. The worst part for victims is that physically removing oneself from a live bullying situation is no longer a surefire way to stop abuse.

What can be done about this, and how can you cope? It is not easy, but there are many strategies to

Because teenagers often have their mobile devices nearby, cyberbullying can occur at any time of the day. This can mean a seemingly endless cycle of daily and nightly abuse.

prevent, deal with, and even do away with cyberbullying on a case-by-case basis. There are even movements by school communities lately to rally around victims. Coping with cyberbullying is a new frontier of modern life.

CHAPTER ONE

A Digital Age Issue

According to a report released in 2015 by the Pew Research Center, 92 percent of teens say they go online every day. The study reported that 24 percent of teens, defined by this study as those from the ages of thirteen to seventeen, go online "almost constantly." Overall, 56 percent of teens go online multiple times a day, compared to 12 percent who say they go online just once a day. Only 6 percent say they go online just once a week. The catalyst for the constant online connection is the availability of smartphones.

Pew's research showed that nearly 75 percent of teens either own or have access to a smartphone, while only 12 percent say they do not have a mobile device of any type. The research also showed that 91 percent of teens use their mobile devices to go online at least occasionally, and nearly all of these

Research shows that the vast majority of teens have access to the Internet every day via different electronic devices. For all intents and purposes, a big chunk of teens nowadays live online.

teens go online at least once a day. The numbers show that teens who do not go online using a mobile device go online less frequently overall.

Where do all of them flock to online? The study revealed that Facebook, Instagram, and Snapchat are the top social media platforms for teens. Facebook reigns supreme with 71 percent of teens claiming they use the site, while about 50 percent are on Instagram, and 40 percent on Snapchat. But even with these high usage rates, teens are not locked into just one social media platform. In the study, 71 percent report using multiple outlets, including Google+, Twitter, Tumblr, and more.

Social conventions and interactions have changed over the last twenty years, and defining cyberbullying is a modern exercise. Exactly what kind of behaviors count as cyberbullying? Aside from it happening online or via phone or smartphone, what defines cyberbullying? The first step in addressing the problem is identifying it in the first place.

Exclusion

According to social psychologists, the desire to feel included is a basic human need. In a teen's world, this often translates to being popular, or at least not terribly unpopular. Exclusion can be one of the most painful experiences for young people.

Psychologists have pointed out that, for teens, being accepted and included is an important aspect of social life. All is right with the world if someone makes you feel worthwhile on social media.

Just as in the nondigital world, online exclusion can be emotionally hurtful. Many social media sites and applications feature an inner-circle aspect such as a friends list or a group of people who are followed. On Facebook, for example, unfriending—or removing someone from one's list of online friends or contacts—can have just as much impact as ostracism in the real world. Studies have shown that exclusion leads to lowered self-esteem for those who are left out.

Exclusion can take many forms, sometimes in ways that are not explicit or obvious upon first inspection. In online culture, people are expected to respond quickly to messages or e-mails. This assumes that most teens are connected much of the time. If a reply is not perceived as being prompt, it may be viewed as a social misstep, or rudeness.

This can be a two-way street in which perception and reality differ greatly. A popular or well-liked person might feel slighted if another person does not respond to her chats, messages, or texts right away because she is used to others doing what she wants. Meanwhile, someone who is desperate for friendship might be sitting around waiting for others to respond to him and panicking when they don't, even if the other people might be asleep, in the shower, engaged in some other activity, or simply away from their mobile device.

Flaming and Denigration

Flaming is when individuals exchange heated messages in public forums such as a chat room or discussion group. The exchange then escalates into a series of insults known as a flame war. While flaming can occur between two individuals on equal grounds, it may not seem that way to those involved when more people join in on one side versus the other.

Denigration, on the other hand, happens in a more secretive manner. It refers to someone spreading derogatory and false information about an individual through e-mails, messaging, online posts, or other similar methods. Aside from text, the information could be digitally altered photos portraying a target in a hurtful way, an insulting song written about a victim, or other forms of media. Another tradition among some students are slam books, which are passed around among the student body. Some of these are circulated specifically to have students call out specific peers by name and allow others to write nasty comments about each other. Hurtful notes and information left on physical bulletin boards and in chat rooms are other forms of anonymous and semi-anonymous cyberbullying.

Harassment and Cyberstalking

In cyberbullying terms, harassment is repeatedly sending emotionally distressing e-mails, messages, texts, or other forms of electronic communication with the intent to annoy and sometimes alarm a person. These messages serve no purpose other than to harm someone, although they may result in other consequences, intentional and otherwise. For example, repeatedly sending text messages to a cell phone can increase a person's phone bill.

Unlike flame wars, a campaign of harassment is a long-term form of cyberbullying that is more one-sided. Harassment can occur in online gaming as well, where players are more concerned with harassing other players via negative messages than playing the game itself.

Cyberstalking occurs when technology is used to give someone

Cyberstalking can be devastating for a victim. The consistent nature of harassment can make a person feel helpless and cornered at all times.

unwanted attention in an obsessive way. It can often be frightening—most often for girls and women—though anyone can be made to feel highly uncomfortable or fearful for their safety. The National Institute of Justice compares cyberstalking to real-life stalking in that both involve the "pursuit, harassment, or contact of others in an unsolicited fashion." Cyberstalking usually involves the internet, email, chat rooms, and other electronic communication methods. The target can receive numerous messages and images from a cyberstalker, with obscene, hateful, or threatening content. Cyberstalking can escalate to the stalker assuming a false identity to post more content about the victim, or even posing as the victim to solicit responses and email from others online, including the victim's friends and family. Cyberstalkers can even physically appear at a target's residence or workplace. This is often the end result of the authorities not taking such behavior as seriously as they should. Many celebrities and people in the public eye suffer through this, and some have even been stalked and killed.

Impersonation, Outing, and Trickery

Another form of cyberbullying involves the bully pretending to be the victim to send out negative comments meant to harm the victim's reputation. Through

The Bully Project

In 2011, director Lee Hirsch released his documentary Bully to great acclaim. The film brought the bullying crisis even more prominently to the forefront of public attention. The film rode a wave of popular-media coverage of bullied kids and the terrible aftermaths of several real-life tragedies in the news. In some instances, victims even took their own lives.

The film takes a hard, unflinching look at the real consequences of bullying, especially when nothing is done to help a victim. The accounts can be difficult to watch, but they attach names and faces to bullying. Hirsch was careful to not sugarcoat the tortured reality many kids and teens face every day.

The popularity of Bully was leveraged to launch TheBullyProject.com, a website aimed at providing kids and parents with resources to help them deal with bullying. It also encourages people to try and make a difference in the lives of those who have been victimized by bullies. The social action campaign urges people not to look away from bullying, but to transform the lives of kids everywhere. Additionally, it has a goal of reaching ten million kids or more through its 10 Million Kids initiative. The initiative helps educators screen the film for students and teachers alike.

impersonation, the cyberbully can gain access to the victim's personal accounts by stealing passwords or using other dirty tricks. Posing as the victim, the cyberbully can send out messages to the victim's friends and family that will severely harm those relationships. The impersonator can break into a victim's accounts to manipulate someone's web presence in a hurtful and embarrassing way. There are technologies and methods of hacking that can steal another person's password, thus making that person all the more vulnerable to any number of cyberbullying tactics.

Some other forms of cyberbullying include outing and trickery. Outing occurs when personal or private information is shared without permission. For example, a cyberbully could learn about a target's personal life and share that publicly through an email

Rumors and hurtful messages are dangerous online, where they can spread quickly. They can jump easily from online to offline and back on again.

or online post. Information could be a text, a photo, or some other form of media, including documents. A person can even be doxxed, where his or her private phone number and address are revealed to the public. Trickery is the name given to the method a cyberbully would use to get personal information about someone that the person would not have otherwise shared.

A Growing Problem

Various troubling studies conducted internationally show an increase in cyberbullying in a number of nations. The Cyberbullying Research Center conducted research for more than ten years by surveying a random sample of students from middle and high schools in the United States. Subjects were asked if they had ever experienced cyberbullying at some point in their lifetime. While the percentage of students who claimed they had experienced cyberbullying varied from year to year, the overall trend clearly showed an increase in the number of students who had been victimized online or through electronic communication. In May 2007, about 19 percent of students claimed to have been victimized, while in August of 2016 that number jumped to just under 34 percent.

For teen girls, the situation may be even more perilous. A Boston-area study indicated that cyberbullying has spiked more for young women. The Education Development Center reported a jump from 14.6 percent to 21.2 percent of students who experienced cyberbullying over a six-year period ending in 2012. While incidents where boys were the target increased by 3 percent, incidents where girls were the target increased by 10 percent. Additionally, the study showed that the students also were unlikely to seek help, with only one-third of victims sharing their experiences with an adult.

CHAPTER TWO

Identifying a Problem

The first step toward stopping cyberbullying is to identify when it is happening in the first place. Victims display certain behavioral changes that can help signal to others that they are being cyberbullied, while cyberbullies may reveal themselves in entirely different ways. It is also vital and necessary to isolate whether certain young people are more likely to become victims. Whether certain venues (such as social media platforms) by their very nature allow for more or less cyberbullying is important to consider, too.

Telltale Signs of Cyberbullying

The National Crime Prevention Council (NCPC) provides information about the different signs that indicate someone may be a victim of cyberbullying. The organization outlines emotional as well as

A cyberbullying victim may display various symptoms that can help signal to friends and family that help is needed. This may include appearing distracted, preoccupied, or anxious.

social behaviors and academic trends that could point to cyberbully victimization. Some teens are too embarrassed to speak up about their issues. But a teacher, friend, or other person noticing these signs and responding to them may perhaps even save someone's life.

Some emotional signs can include becoming withdrawn or shy, but bullying can also push victims

Cyberbullyng may start online and then continue in real life. It is especially concerning if it leads to physical confrontations or abuse. Of course, virtual bullying hurts emotionally.

into exhibiting aggression. Victims will likely show signs of depression and can become extremely moody and agitated, stressed, and anxious.

Cyberbullying, like all types of harassment, can negatively impact a person's academic life. Victims will begin to lose interest in school and may choose not to go altogether. Some skip classes to avoid those they believe or know to be bullying them online. If they do go to school, they are more likely get into trouble while there. Their interest in school will decline and their grades will suffer.

At home, victims will attempt to escape the cyberbully and suddenly stop using the computer. Withdrawal from technology is one big signal that someone is being cyberbullied. This includes withdrawal from smartphones or other electronic devices. Regular, necessary activities such as eating or sleeping will be affected, too. Some victims report being plagued by nightmares. Their circle of friends will change, as will their preference in activities.

Activities victims used to enjoy doing no longer bring the same joy as before. In some cases, victims may even hurt themselves, engaging in activities such as cutting. In the most tragic scenarios, victims attempt suicide. Sometimes they succeed.

The NCPC acknowledges that a cyberbullying victim may also suffer other types of victimization such as physical bullying or physically abusive relationships. It strongly suggests that victim service providers be well trained to recognize the signs and how to help, especially if a victim's situation is complicated.

Stopbullying.gov, a website managed by the United States Department of Health and Human Services, warns that victims of bullying are also more likely than their peers to seek to escape and may dull their emotional pain by engaging in risky behaviors, especially substance abuse. This includes consuming alcohol or abusing prescription and illegal drugs. Such behaviors are more likely to exacerbate hopelessness and depression, pushing a person even deeper into an emotional downward spiral.

How Can You Recognize a Cyberbully?

Along with signs a victim may display, the NCPC outlined several signs that could help identify when people might be cyberbullies themselves. Cyberbullies may turn off a computer screen or stop using the computer whenever someone comes near or approaches them. Additionally, while using the computer or smartphone, a cyberbully may act nervous or jumpy. These signs point to secretive behavior. Computer and smartphone usage time can even increase to excessive amounts, and cyberbullies will become upset or angry when their time with their devices is reduced or taken away. Some cyberbullies even get addicted to the adrenaline rush of seeing the effects of their bad behavior.

The online Cyberbullying Research Center has noted other behaviors characteristic of cyberbullies. These include using their devices at all hours of the night, laughing excessively at something that is happening online, using multiple online accounts or one that is not their own, and appearing overly conceited about their technological skills and abilities. Offline, cyberbullies may hang out with troublemakers and consistently demonstrate callousness or insensitivity toward other teens. They may even become increasingly withdrawn from family.

It Can Happen to Anyone

Cyberbullying's targets are not restricted to a certain type of person or a specific group. Of course, ethnicity, gender identity, or reputation are reasons why a cyberbully may latch onto someone. But it is

Anyone can be a victim of cyberbullying no matter what their race, gender, or age. Bullies come in many forms, too. A fight or physical altercation can spark cyberbullying, too.

a mistake to think that they would not pick someone else entirely in another situation. Rather, many people of all ages, races, gender or gender identifications, religions, or other identifying characteristic are vulnerable to attack online, where anonymity is common. It can happen to anyone. Sometimes a bully does not single a person out for anything that person does. Bullying can be completely arbitrary. It also can be more about the issues the bully faces and less about the victim's personality, lifestyle, identity, or interests.

To bullies, a victim could be someone who just happens to be available or someone who they think will not defend themselves. Similarly, Internet users can easily join in when many others make comments about a video or photo that has gone viral. While they may not see much harm in adding one more hurtful comment to the others, the viciousness does not diminish for the victim. This is seen in cases where a group of people, such as a

Studies conducted on cyberbullying reveal that girls and women are at higher risk of being cyberbullying victims than boys and men.

class or team, engage in bullying and display signs of a mob mentality.

There do tend to be differences in how much different people get cyberbullied. Someone could be targeted based on their gender identity, age, race, or religion. Any kind of difference that makes someone stand out can make him or her a target.

Whatever the impetus is the fact remains that many cyberbullies and their victims know each other, sometimes even very well. Some might be ex-best friends or even current friends, since some cyberbullies harass people secretly. Consider also that random harassment that perhaps is not repeated is different in nature than sustained, repeated cyberbullying.

Differences in Gender

Studies have shown that girls are equally or more likely to be involved in cyberbullying. According to researchers Justin Patchin and

Sameer Hinduja of the Cyberbullying Research Center, of thirteen different studies, eight found that girls are more frequently victims, while three showed boys as more frequent victims. The other two studies found no difference by gender. Overall, the studies showed that about 22 percent of girls reported being victims of cyberbullying compared to almost 20 percent of boys.

Patchin and Hinduja also noted that the studies showed that boys are more likely than girls to admit to being a cyberbully. Of the thirteen studies conducted, eleven showed that boys were more likely to engage in cyberbullying behavior, and the other two studies showed no difference. Overall, a little more than 14 percent of girls and almost 19 percent of boys admit to being a cyberbully.

Girls have had more experience with indirect, or nonphysical, forms of aggression. Secondly, adolescent girls who bully routinely choose to use nonphysical methods to exclude or hurt others. Both of these behaviors are easily carried out through technology.

Many people report being targeted by cyberbullies because of their sexual orientation or how they self-identify their gender. According to *Psychology Today*, in an online survey of young people between the ages of eleven and twenty-two, about 54 percent of lesbian, gay, bisexual, and transgender children said that they had been cyberbullied within thirty days of the survey. The report also showed that almost half the respondents

An online survey seems to indicate that over half of lesbian, gay, bisexual, and transgender young people had been recently cyberbullied, within the previous thirty days.

were depressed as a result of being cyberbullied, and 26 percent admitted to having suicidal thoughts.

Difference by Grade Level and Race

Students will experience a different amount of cyberbullying in their middle school years compared to other years at school. According to Patchin and Hinduja, the peak of cyberbullying occurs in middle school, while other studies show that it carries on through high school. In grades eight through ten, cyberbullying tends to level off, while eleventh and twelfth graders show an increase in this type of activity. For offenders, the studies show similar numbers, although a progressively higher percentage of students admit to cyberbullying in the eleventh and twelfth grades.

Cyberbullying tactics differ among races, but generally all races are targeted at comparable rates. Some suggest that because of the anonymity of cyberspace, bullies tend to act out in ways that are not culturally acceptable in the real world. Furthermore, these same groups may feel that repercussions are minimized when actions are carried out digitally rather than physically. Cyberbullies doing it for the fun of it get a thrill at breaking social conventions, while they also do not see the real-world effects of how they hurt people.

Bullying's Tools of the Trade

Just as Internet technologies have evolved from slow dial-up modems to fast Wi-Fi signals and wired networks, bullying has evolved along with the digital age. Compounding the disturbing trend, social media has given kids, some under the age of thirteen, the ability to connect with one another in ways unimaginable to people just a generation ago. Cyberbullying and related antisocial behaviors such as trolling on the Internet have spread to nearly all online forums, news sites, social media networks, and anywhere people can chime in with their thoughts and opinions.

To combat the issue, several of the most popular social media sites and applications have introduced technological solutions. Twitter and Instagram enable users to filter out abusive comments, as well as block trolls and other abusive accounts.

Meanwhile, Facebook created a bullying prevention hub to provide a place for teens and parents to talk about cyberbullying. Apps such as STOPit and BullyBox give kids a way to report

(continued on the next page)

> *(continued from the previous page)*
>
> abuse, plus Bully Block records bullying as it happens. According to the Christian Science Monitor, cyber-psychologist Mary Aiken introduced the "Aiken algorithm," which can detect bullying and automatically alert kids and parents.

It Can Happen Anywhere

In a sense, the Internet is everywhere. Young people can connect at home, school, the library, and on their personal mobile devices. Unfortunately, this means that a cyberbully can reach them anywhere, no matter how safe a space seems. The bullies of yesteryear could not chase or continue to harass their victims who escaped to their homes, or left for holidays, summer vacation, camp, and family trips. That is no longer an option for victims of cyberbullying. The second they go online, where many young people conduct much of their social life and interactions, a hurtful or harassing message or post awaits them.

Social Media Platforms

Of all internet-based phenomena, social media sites have become the most important fixtures in the lives of modern adolescents and even pre-adolescents. Several have risen and fallen in popularity (or been shut down), such as MySpace, Xanga, Vine, and LiveJournal, while others such as the Canadian site Nexopia still boast a dedicated core of users. One of the most popular sites, Facebook, has its own culture and features that cyberbullies can take advantage of to hurt other users.

From 2010 to 2011, one million children reported being cyberbullied, including the receipt of harassment and threats. With over five million users discovered to be under ten years old, the risk to youthful users is apparent. A survey conducted by antibullying charity Ditch the Label found that Facebook, Twitter, and Ask.FM are the most common social networks for cyberbullying. More than half of young people who use Facebook say they have been cyberbullied on the network. In comparison, 28 percent of young people say they have experienced cyberbullying on Twitter, and 26 percent on Ask.FM. Another study in 2015 found that Instagram was more popular than Facebook among middle-schoolers, according to the Megan Meier Foundation.

Email and Instant Messaging

With smartphones, cyberbullying can occur via instant messaging applications, in emails and direct messages in Facebook and applications, and through texting. Some types of communication are conducive to particular types of cyberbullying. Flaming, for example, is more common in public forums or message boards, while harassment is usually more common in private communications such as text messages or emails. Cyberbullies can use instant messaging to harass others by sending out mean or hurtful messages. They can also impersonate a victim by changing their screen name to closely resemble or even be identical to their target's screen name. Under this false persona, a cyberbully then sends out messages, images, or other media in order to harm the victim's relationships and reputation.

Because of its ease of use and the ability to quickly send communications to large numbers of recipients, email remains a popular medium for cyberbullying. Harassing emails are just the tip of the iceberg. Victims might be signed up for inappropriate or obscene websites and mailing lists or have their address stolen or mimicked. For example, if someone's email address is Mary .Johnson@gmail.com, a cyberbully could send a note from MaryJohnson@gmail.com (note the dropped period), thereby pretending to be the original address owner. Many people automatically reply to emails without carefully scrutinizing the sender. It might be a long time before that person's friends get wise to this form of trickery.

Bullying text messages can be particularly harmful because users often keep their mobile devices close at hand. Some people are rarely without them. Cases of cyberbullying in which teens receive hundreds or even thousands of hurtful texts are not unheard of.

Gaming

In online gaming, cyberbullying comes in the form of "torment, humiliation, and belittling" according to Sally Black of Saint Joseph University. Gaming cyberbullies are known as griefers, and they exert their aggressive behavior by lurking in online multiplayer video games and bullying other players by tormenting and thwarting them. Black says that victims will be trapped by griefers, who will then proceed to attack the victim throughout the game.

CHAPTER THREE

Pushing Back on Cyberbullying

Cyberbullying can leave victims feeling helpless and cornered. Any course of action they choose to take feels pointless and seems as if it would lead to only more bullying. It can feel like a downward spiral and lead to a person feeling he or she is losing control of life. However, there are ways to properly handle the situation. Some may be difficult and require some courage. But pushing back against cyberbullying safely and ethically, by themselves and with the help of friends, trusted adults, and whole communities, can help victims overcome, heal, and even begin to help others.

What To Do When Cyberbullied

The media attention being paid to high-profile bullying cases has cultivated an atmosphere where teens are thankfully more willing to come forward with their personal stories and experiences.

Opening up about being bullied online or otherwise can feel pretty daunting. However, the road to addressing the situation usually won't present itself without confiding in someone.

This is also true because of various well-publicized antibullying efforts being waged by organizations, school districts, individual schools, educators and administrators, and students themselves—especially victims. There is far more knowledge about the subject and awareness of it than ever before. Armed with information and strategies, people can better combat cyberbullying.

The first thing researchers and professionals recommend doing is talking about being cyberbullied with a trusted adult. This could be a parent, a teacher, a counselor, or someone similar. When no adult is available, cyberbullying victims are encouraged to talk to a friend whom they can trust. The important thing is to avoid keeping the situation a secret. In addition to being able to express their feelings, victims give their loved ones and friends the chance to provide support and perhaps begin the process of making the problem go away.

For initial instances or isolated incidents, many people recommend simply ignoring the bully. Cyberbullies may not continue harassing a victim if there is no response, so victims are encouraged to not interact with the instigator. Cyberbullies are looking for a reaction from their targets. As with internet trolls, the idea is to simply deny them the thing they are looking for—a reaction from their victim.

Along the same lines, cyberbullying targets should avoid retaliating, or seeking revenge on the bully by carrying out a similar attack. Retaliation also can create a cycle where a bully attacks, the victim responds with another attack, and things endlessly go back and forth. The violence and level of attack could escalate, making the situation much worse than before and leaving the original problem unresolved.

In some cases, a victim may set in motion events in which the bully may try to attack the victim in person or escalate the situation in other ways that can cause physical harm.

Additionally, retaliating could get victims in trouble, even though they did not begin the cycle themselves. A good idea is to stay calm and avoid reacting out of anger or fear. When cyberbullies elicit a strong response from a target, they will often boast about this as a victory later. They may even post screenshots of victims' responses for laughs. A response is almost sure to prolong the situation even more.

Stopping Bullying on the Spot

Often, simply ignoring cyberbullying does not work. The next step, then, would be to tell the person to stop. The victim should clearly state that the bully's actions are hurtful. It's important to retain a respectful tone and avoid a response that could be misconstrued as retaliatory. Responding aggressively may make things worse. Respond seriously and firmly. Professionals believe it is important for victims to voice their feelings either in public or private, as long as they make the point that they will not tolerate hurtful behaviors. When responding to cyberbullies, it is important to not only be respectful but also hold those

A bullying situation may be cut short if one confronts a tormenter in person—safely, obviously. The line between standing up for oneself and starting fights can be a thin one, of course.

people accountable for their actions. Responses must be constructive and clear. If the situation escalates and it is necessary for others to intervene, the victim also has proof that he or she did not seek out this person's attention or prolong the interaction.

Another strategy might be to simply laugh off the harassment. It could be possible that the cyberbully is not aware that what he or she sees as humorous is actually hurtful. Jokes can be taken too far, and recognizing when this happens can be the most productive path to end the situation.

Keep Your Evidence

As cyberbullying occurs, victims should save all the evidence they can. This means saving messages from all sources such as Facebook, Reddit, or other websites, or at least screenshots of the offending activity. Text messages should be saved and all the evidence printed out, too, if possible. Any of these materials can possibly be useful later when explaining the situation to adults. Hopefully it does not come to this, but such evidence might prove useful to law enforcement if the bullying escalates.

Block Away

Most websites give users the option to block others from contacting them or engaging in other unwelcome activity. Making it impossible for a cyberbully to make contact is a good initial step. Victims can, for example, use Facebook's tools to keep the cyberbully from engaging them. Chat applications such as Google Chat give users the option to stay hidden so another user never sees them online. Mobile phones allow users to block text or phone calls from unwanted callers. If a site's blocking tools are ineffective, the victims can file an official complaint or report with the website. Facebook, YouTube, and Google make reporting cyberbullying relatively simple. Many websites have terms and conditions of service that protect their users from harassment. Victims can also enlist telecommunications providers to stop bullies. Service providers have the ability to block certain numbers from making contact.

Mass emails or texts from a cyberbully about someone else should be deleted immediately. Passing along the harmful image or text is exactly what the cyberbully wants and only exacerbates the problem. Spreading content coming from a cyberbully becomes part of the problem. Anyone receiving these types of messages should let the sender know that passing

Caitlin Prater-Haacke

In 2014, Caitlin Prater-Haacke, an eleventh grader in Alberta, Canada, noticed an alarming Facebook post on her page. The message urged her to kill herself. Alarmingly, it looked like she had posted it herself. Later, it would be revealed that someone broke into her locker at school and used her iPad to impersonate her on Facebook. According to the Toronto Sun, this person changed her status, encouraging her to die.

How Caitlin chose to respond, however, was surprising, but in a much more positive way. According to an account from the Christian Science Monitor, she chose not to let her cyberbully discourage her or get her down. Instead, she wrote positive messages on eight hundred notes intended to encourage and inspire her classmates. She left them around her school, leaving a positive message on every locker. Some of the notes read, "You're beautiful," while others encouraged readers to, "Love yourself" or stated "You're awesome." Her unknown cyberbully received a note, too.

However, she was met with another roadblock when the school reprimanded her. The school considered her project littering. Her mother was outraged. She wondered how the school could ignore the cyberbullying but decide to punish a

(continued on the next page)

(continued from the previous page)

student who was doing something to help others. But even the school's response did not deter Caitlin from her goal of spreading positivity in the face of cyberbullying.

Caitlin's hometown was more supportive. The mayor led a new antibullying campaign called "Positive Post-It Day," which encourages people to follow Caitlin's lead by leaving anonymous positive notes of kindness on October 9. In an interview with the Toronto Sun, Caitlin said, "Bullying is not necessarily addressed, and people get really down about it. I wanted to do something positive—it was about due time."

along embarrassing messages or photos of someone else is worthy of disgust.

In extreme cases where safety is threatened, the police should be contacted. Either when the victim feels in danger or if a friend sees that the situation is headed toward a dangerous path, law enforcement needs to be involved to provide safety. In the meantime, an adult should be informed for protection while awaiting the police.

Many cyberbullies have an inability to empathize with others and have no feelings about bullying others online. It may be second nature for them to gang up on someone.

Are You the Bully?

Psychologists have considered why people become cyberbullies and have concluded that there are complex factors that play into it. Research has suggested that cyberbullies tend to have less empathy than the average person. According to *Psychology Today*, 40 percent of cyberbullies had no feelings after bullying someone online, while 16 percent felt guilty. Some cyberbullies said that their behavior made them feel "funny, popular, and powerful."

When students believe others are bullying online, they are more likely to engage in similar behavior themselves. A person's home life could sway him or her, too. Cyberbullies are more likely to have poor or dysfunctional relationships with their parents, and an abusive home is more likely to produce abusive kids. Parents' failure to pay attention to their kid's activities can factor in also.

Sometimes cyberbullies don't realize that they are harassing someone. Nevertheless, certain actions are signs of cyberbullying, whether they are done intentionally to hurt someone or not.

There are other less obvious behaviors that can be classified as cyberbullying. If a student knows that someone is being cyberbullied but does not intervene or seek help, one could consider that cyberbullying, too. The same can be said for laughing

If you are wondering if the way someone is engaging with you online is abusive—or even if you think you might be crossing a line—it is a good bet your friends can help you figure it out.

along with friends at someone else being victimized or participating by reposting, forwarding, or piling on in any way.

Free Speech?

One of the core rights of Americans is that of freedom of speech. From criticizing local sports teams to judging politicians, this freedom is very broad. While the content of most nonviolent speech is protected by law, there are restrictions. One can criticize the football team but cannot repeatedly call the quarterback at three in morning to do so. Likewise, while students are free to voice their views to an extent, there are prohibitions on disturbing the learning environment. US courts have approved of special restrictions in schools to maintain an appropriate school climate.

Cyberbullying was singled out in 2014 by the New York State Court of Appeals. As noted by Patchin and Hinduja, the court stated, "Cyberbullying is not conceptually immune from government regulation, so we may assume ... that the First Amendment permits the prohibition of cyberbullying directed at children, depending on how that activity is defined."

In the case that brought about this decision, a local cyberbullying law in Albany County, New York, was declared invalid. The court argued that the law was written too broadly and violated First Amendment

Cyberbullies are not usually strangers, especially when it comes to long-term bouts of extreme harassment. Victims often personally know who is harassing them.

free speech protections. The court argued, "The provision would criminalize a broad spectrum of speech outside the popular understanding of cyberbullying, including ... a telephone conversation meant to annoy an adult."

Victim and Bully Relationship

Most cyberbullying occurs between people who know each other. About 84 percent of cyberbullying victims were found to know their cyberbully, according to one study conducted in 2009 referenced by Patchin and Hinduja. In contrast, anywhere from 7 percent to 13 percent of cyberbullying victims did not know their cyberbully, depending on the study cited.

Patchin and Hinduja also noted that more than 30 percent of young people involved in cyberbullying were both victims and cyberbullies themselves. One of the biggest reasons young people give for being a cyberbully is revenge—retaliation against their own tormentor. Many who admit to being a cyberbully feel justified in their actions because they feel they were wronged first. In some cases, someone bullied earlier may take out their frustrations on their own innocent victim later.

Myths & FACTS

Myth: Cyberbullying is not as serious as bullying in person.

Fact: Because the social lives of many young people today occur largely online, cyberbullying can be as bad, or even worse, than bullying in person.

Myth: The anonymity provided by the internet is a new feature of bullying.

Fact: Young people have been bullied anonymously long before the internet era—for example, via rumors and other harassment campaigns.

Myth: Turning off one's mobile device or computer will stop cyberbullying.

Fact: Cyberbullies can still circulate hurtful messages on their end, and damage can still be done even if the victim is not aware of it.

CHAPTER FOUR

Seeking Help

Internet technologies facilitate cyberbullying, but can also provide help for victims. As the issue has gained attention, various concerned young people, organizations, and others have stepped up to help connect victims (and cyberbullies) with help and counseling, online communities that can help, and various sites that provide antibullying strategies and coping mechanisms. There are many websites to choose from, many of which cater to particular audiences.

Not Alone

Victims should realize that they are not alone. Today there are a greater number of people ready to offer their help and services to anyone who needs them. The Cybersmile Foundation is an organization that offers help via multiple platforms. Teens can call, email, or connect via Facebook. Its twenty-four-hour Twitter helpline was recognized by Twitter as one of the most trusted resources.

There are many resources online that can connect someone with discrete, professional support. There are even those specifically for people who are being bullied because of a disability.

Itis particularly well known for providing instant advice in response to specific queries and situations. Cybersmile cofounder Dan Raisbeck tells *US News & World Report*, "If someone is having problems, they can come get some confidential feedback from us, from one of our advisers."

Putting a Price on Being Cyberbullied

A victim's finances can be affected by cyber-harassment, too. For example, a cyberbully may blow up someone's phone with texts and incur data overages. Additionally, cyberbullying victims could also be subject to wrongful termination from their places of employment if their bullies keep calling or bothering them on the job. Rumors and fake emergency calls perpetrated by cyberbullies have also resulted in victims experiencing false arrest or unwanted attention from police and other authorities. Absenteeism, including lost time from work, can occur if the harassment affects their stress and anxiety levels. Those who are stressed out or otherwise incapacitated by their situation may seek help through psychiatric care. This may cost money that neither a victim nor their families can afford.

Telling one's story can help with healing. The site Wordswound.org provides teens with the opportunity to do just that. Victims can share their stories and experiences, while others seeking help can read about them and learn how to cope with their own situations.

Cyberbullying expert Justin Patchin says that teens do not always feel comfortable speaking with their parents about their personal troubles, so confiding in someone who understands what they are going through is vitally important. The anonymity these venues provide is also attractive to troubled youth. Websites such as Cybersmile, Wordswound.org, and others like them could give teens the emotional outlet they desperately need.

Who Else Can Help?

Depending on the situation, there are different types of assistance victims can seek. If the cyberbullying involves someone in their class or school, a teacher, a school counselor, or the principal may be the first line of defense. Of course, cyberbullying would not be the problem it is if seeking such help were truly so simple. Often, it is the stigma of being a victim, and the fear that few will believe their story, that prevents people from coming forward. It takes a lot of courage for victims in any situation to come forward. They may also fear retaliation from the bully or bullies who are punished. Or they may fear that their bullies will not get punished at all. Sometimes, with little proof, their efforts may be in vain.

If a student or her parents are not getting results from the educators or administrators close to the situation, they may seek assitance from a school superintendent or even a state's department of education. Situations ideal for this type of treatment include when a school is ignoring situations based on race, nationality, gender, disability, or religion. Many have realized that ignoring cries of help from those bullied is a surefire way to be investigated for violating student rights. Available federal-level offices include the US Department of Education, US Office for Civil Rights, and the US Department of Justice, Civil Rights Division. For immediate issues where someone is in harm's way or a crime is in progress, people should call 911 to get emergency help from police.

Reach Out for Help

For victims who feel hopeless, helpless, or suicidal, there is a toll-free number for the National Suicide

Students are encouraged to reach out to a trusted adult for help and guidance when confronted with cyberbullying. This individual might be a favorite teacher, for instance.

Prevention Lifeline for immediate help. The lifeline can be reached online, too. The National Suicide Prevention Lifeline is available for crisis counseling and mental health referrals at any time of the day or night. Those who suffer from pre-existing conditions such as bipolar disorder should seek immediate help once they begin to engage in self-harm in response to cyberbullying, as they may be more vulnerable to its dangerous effects. Self-harm also includes self-destructive behaviors such as drug and alcohol abuse. Severe depression and suicide are, tragically, too-frequent outcomes in cyberbullying cases that must be addressed quickly and with sensitivity.

The Trevor Project

Predating most instances of cyberbullying, the Trevor Project was founded in 1998 by the creators of the short film *Trevor*. The film is about a boy with a secret crush on his male schoolmate and what happened when his secret was discovered. It went on to win an Academy Award, but more important, the film led to the creation of the Trevor Project. The organization provides services for young lesbian, gay, bisexual, and transgender people between the ages of thirteen and twenty-four. Services include crisis intervention and suicide prevention such as the Trevor Lifeline available by phone; TrevorChat, for instant messaging with trained volunteer counselors and TrevorText, where LGBTQ youth can text with a trained counselor. The Trevor Project also offers suicide prevention training and resources, as well as a safe social networking community for LGBTQ youths. Their Trevor Ambassadors are volunteer groups located throughout the United States.

STOMP Out Bullying!

STOMP Out Bullying offers a HelpChat Line for young people between the ages of thirteen and twenty-four who are victims of bullying or cyberbullying. The free and confidential chat line assists cyberbullying victims and those at risk for suicide. Targeted specifically at youth, HelpChat's goal is to help cyberbullying victims cope with stress and make positive decisions. The trained volunteers are careful to help those feeling distressed and needing emotional support, without passing any judgment.

Volunteers ask about the victim's safety. Specifically, they try to discover victims' emotions and thoughts regarding their situation and whether callers are suffering from depression or having suicidal thoughts. The HelpChat counselor will also help explore available options moving forward. In urgent situations, the volunteer counselor can explain how to access emergency services.

In addition to accessing confidential counseling, teens can find places to post or publish their stories of cyberbullying, as a way to cope, through online antibullying sites.

Teens Against Bullying

The PACER Center helps bullied youth who are also disabled. Their National Bullying Prevention Center focuses on getting young people the help they need when faced with a bully. The PACER Center's Teens Against Bullying was created by and intended for middle school and high school students. It is an online resource that teens can use to learn ways to address bullying and to have a place where they can voice their feelings. The website posts stories from other teens who have experienced bullying. The center's free online resources also include materials for parents, to help them learn how they can guide their children through difficult times. They also post helpful ways to spark a discussion with students and children about cyberbullying and how harmful it can be.

Resources for Parents and Teachers

There are several resources available for adults who want to help. Parents and

Some young people might be mortified at the prospect of confiding in their parents to get help or advice on cyberbullying. But it is likely the best option that will help the fastest.

teachers, for example, can use these websites and organizations to better understand what a young person is going through. It may not always be obvious or easy for parents to help their child. Luckily, these professionals can get the victims the help they need.

Gay Lesbian Straight Education Network

The Gay Lesbian Straight Education Network (GLSEN) aims to improve the education system for lesbian, gay, bisexual, transgender, or queer students who are targets of bullying and cyberbullying. According to GLSEN, pronounced "glisten," eight out of ten LGBTQ students are harassed at school each year just for being who they are. Founded in 1990, the once small group has expanded into a national organization.

GLSEN's resources include guides for educators such as an LGBTQ-inclusive curriculum. They have a goal of raising awareness about the plight of LGBTQ students and shine a light on the ways that people can hurt these students without even knowing it. The organization does not provide its own call center or online chat to help young people in need. Instead it provides the contact information for the Trevor Project's many services.

CyberBully Hotline

The CyberBully Hotline is available to both victims and their parents. The service accepts anonymous calls and texts from either victims or their parents to begin a prevention program. Once an incident has been reported, school leaders are then contacted.

They can then respond to each report directly. The reports are tracked and managed online.

The system has to be put into place with the help of the CyberBully Hotline staff. After a school is given a custom local number and those involved go through a training program, parents and students will then be able to file reports of cyberbullying incidents. Messages with certain keywords like "gun" or "suicide" are flagged as high priority.

Interventions

Traditional punishment methods such as expulsion and suspension may not be the most effective way to curtail bullying. New attitudes and research on the topic suggest that direct interventions carried out by different people can address cyberbullying in less punitive and more constructive and productive ways. Of course, most everyone would agree that someone who is violent, dangerous, or particularly vicious in cyberbullying should be punished in some way. Still, many educators, and even antibullying activists, believe each case should be judged on its own merits, and that the rush to enact zero tolerance policies in schools might be doing more harm than good.

Positive Peer Pressure

One group of people that can help positively modify bullying behavior is students themselves. Many students indirectly involved with bullying might not even realize they are doing something wrong. They could look the other way when they witness a cyberbullying situation, or they could encourage bullies to carry on with their bad behavior.

Interventions can be held to show students how this kind of indirect behavior plays a role in cyberbullying and how their actions can either enable or help combat cyberbullying. An interesting suggestion by professionals is to enter the bullies into leadership roles with younger students. Under adult supervision, the bullies can be asked to mentor younger students with the idea that they will begin to carry out more positive interactions with others. Former bullies, who long for acceptance or an outlet, could even transform into mentors and learn leadership.

CHAPTER FIVE

Prevention and Treatment

There are a number of ways to confront cyberbullying in a smart, productive way. But is there a way to stop cyberbullying before it happens? Those who have been through it themselves can turn the experience into something positive and, in turn, save others from the same heartache and headaches. They can help victims, create safe spaces and groups and contribute to appropriate, sensible antibullying policies at schools and in online spaces.

Prevention Strategies

Many young people who bully may have things going on in their personal lives that cause them to lash out in hurtful ways. Underlying issues can include skills deficits, anxiety, aggression, impulsivity, and depression. Adults can help adolescents address certain issues before they manifest in negative activities such as posting hateful messages online or harassing victims. If an adult notices a child feeling hopeless or displaying signs of depression, then there is a chance the bully-victim cycle can be interrupted before it begins.

There are many strategies that people can try to prevent cyberbullying. Each has its own strengths and focuses on one of the many facets that go into cyberbullying. There is no guarantee that what works in one situation will work in another. There are different strategies that focus on separate aspects of a teen's life including family, community, friends, and school.

Anger Management

According to many studies, anger is a significant predictor of behavioral issues in young people, including cyberbullying. Anger is a normal emotion that everyone feels, so it should not be looked at as something to be feared or punished. The danger, however, is when that anger is projected onto others by being mean or hurtful. Professionals agree that anger management strategies are important for everyone, especially for young people still learning how to process emotions. When teens are feeling angry, they should talk through their emotions to manage them rather than letting their feelings control them.

A sensitive and perceptive teacher or administrator may recognize a student's anger as a symptom of a deeper problem, like cyberbullying. Aggression can be a cry for help.

Anger management does not come naturally to everyone. It is something many people have to learn. People can be angry without even realizing that they are angry or really knowing what triggered their anger in the first place. There are different anger triggers for each person and different warning signs.

For example, some people get frustrated prior to becoming angry, while others lash out by disrespecting those around them. The moments when a young person's anger is triggered can be a teaching moment. As the anger is rising, the young person should be asked what he or she is feeling and how to handle these emotions.

Working on Perception

Often, rather than being seen as dangerous, hurtful, or mean-spirited, bullies are instead rewarded with popularity and an elevated social status. Bullies claim to feel good about themselves, and other students rate bullies as more popular, athletic, and

Bullies are sometimes rewarded by their peers for their bad behavior. Working to change the perception of bullying can help both the victim and the bully.

attractive. Being aggressive is seen as a positive by others. The unfortunate rewards of cyberbullying reveal a major hurdle to preventing students from being victimized online. To combat cyberbullying, the activity must continue to be stigmatized and deglamorized. It begins with each student recognizing that cyberbully behavior is unacceptable and not to be rewarded.

Rather than suspending or expelling a cyberbully from school, one strategy instead takes the cyberbully through a course with a therapist. The one-on-one course teaches the student about bullying and redefines what bullying behavior really means. The course comes from analyzing the results of studies showing that group interventions are less helpful methods in preventing aggression in young people. In the end, the main goal is to affect and change the culture of how cyberbullies are perceived by others and by themselves.

Teens Take a Stand

In 2014, more than three thousand students at six Tuscaloosa, Alabama, middle schools were given the tools and resources to combat bullying and cyberbullying themselves. Resulting from a public relations campaign by University of Alabama students and months of research and planning, the antibullying program successfully reduced the number of bullying incident reports in all participating schools. Part of a larger program aimed at preventing bullying, the campaign was the second phase of the Tuscaloosa City Schools' Harassment Awareness Learning Together, or HALT, program.

The University of Alabama students held weekly activities with the middle school students. They held mock-bullying scenarios to show students how to properly react to bullying scenarios, all within a safe environment. Regarding prevention, students were asked to design their own plans to stop bullying. They created antibullying stickers for students to wear and created posters that provided helpful tips for victims.

For one week, they had an "I Care" campaign that encouraged students to be more engaged in preventing bullying. Students were asked to write anonymous positive notes for a different classmate every day of the week. There were stickers, banners, and posters for "I Care" week, and many featured fill-in-the-blank messages such as, "I can invite _____ to sit with me." The blank messages were designed for students to interact and participate in the campaign.

The program's success has been attributed to raising the level of student engagement. The students were given a positive viewpoint in addition to specific moves that they could make in their own lives.

Talking It Out

A simple tool to prevent cyberbullying is to talk about it. Students need to know what cyberbullying is in the first place, so speaking to counselors, teachers, and other professionals is a great way to learn how to identify a potentially hazardous situation. Knowing what to look for will better equip students to stop cyberbullying before it begins. They also may learn how to ask trusted adults how to handle harassment and how to stay safe. Communication lines should always remain open because cyberbullying prevention cannot be confined to a single conversation. Having

Talking it out with a trusted adult can help immensely in dealing with cyberbullying. Enlist the wisdom that only years of experience can provide, even if the adult may not be that internet savvy.

a relationship with adults one trusts makes it easier to ask them for help later. This can be established even by asking for advice about fairly innocuous things, such as classes or extracurricular activities, or simply discussing how the day is going.

When speaking with adults about cyberbullying, there are many questions that can be discussed. These can be about why people bully others, what adults can do to help, how young people should handle such situations, and whether they have experienced such harassment personally.

Be More Than a Bystander

Young people have the power to help prevent cyberbullying by doing more than standing idly by while someone else is suffering. Bystanders do not get involved in a situation. They actively decide to maintain their distance. This could be because they are afraid to become a victim themselves or for some other personal reason. There are simple ways to combat the temptation to be a bystander.

Leading by example is a good way to show others the correct way to behave and how to treat others respectfully. Students could discourage others from cyberbullying behavior and actively participate in antibullying campaigns and projects. Others can be encouraged to follow along and participate in these same projects or join similar groups or organizations. Antibullying posters can be made and displayed at school. Simply sharing stories can make a difference in the lives of others.

Another method young people can try to prevent cyberbullying is to make friends with the victim. A simple act of kindness can be an effective way to show the victim that he or she is not alone. Instead of standing by, a student could spend time with the victim by eating lunch or studying together. If a student shares a similar interest with the victim, such as a sport, game, or hobby, they can pass time together engaged in those those activities.

If the victim wants to share his or her feelings about the situation, it is important to be a good listener. Letting the person talk it out will relieve some of the personal stress, and it gives the student an opportunity to provide advice and encouragement. Instead of

A good friend can provide the support a victim desperately needs to help, but it is important to allow the victim to work through their issues at their own pace.

standing by, students can also text or call the victim, letting the person know that the situation is not cool and they are there for support.

Of course, it is always important to respect victims' wishes. They may not want to be friends or prefer to be alone. Even if they accept some gestures of friendship, it is up to them and them alone as to how much they are willing to share or how they will confide in any friend or acquaintance. In other words, be patient and respectful.

Another strategy—and one that not many people think of—is to try befriending the cyberbully. The bully could be having his or her own personal issues that are manifesting in harmful ways and negatively affecting others. Similar to befriending the victim, this tactic encourages students to spend time with the cyberbully and share a mutual interest. If the bully is having personal problems and decides to share them, listening to them could help relieve the bully of some emotional baggage and contribute to ceasing the harassment of others. This would also be a good time to lead by example and show the cyberbully the proper way to interact with and treat others.

10 Great Questions to Ask a School Counselor

1. What is the difference between traditional bullying and cyberbullying?

2. Should parents and the legal system be involved when someone is cyberbullied?

3. What can the school do to help prevent cyberbullying?

4. What should students do if they witness cyberbullying?

5. Will the victim's computer/mobile device be taken away?

6. What steps can the school take when a student is cyberbullied?

7. What programs are there to help victims recover?

8. Is there a place where students can go to speak with other victims?

9. What are the common behaviors that are the result of cyberbullying?

10. Why do people cyberbully others?

CHAPTER SIX

Bouncing Back

After dealing with cyberbullying, how does one go about returning to normal life? Recovering from any kind of abuse often involves finding long-term healing solutions. This means being able to move on from what happened and rising above the diminished self-esteem and confidence that cyberbullying can bring about. It is about learning how to feel good about oneself again. Rather than feeling defeated by negativity, recovering is also about feeling empowered and able to face the situation were it to happen again.

Serious Consequences

Cyberbullying is a serious matter. Those who feel traumatized by it and do not seek help are risking long-term problems that will be harder to address in the future. Every child and young person deserves to live happily and safely, both in their everyday life and in their virtual, digital dealings.

Not dealing with a cyberbullying situation can lead someone to suffer bouts of depression and loneliness, even for a long time after the incidents in question.

For its victims, the consequences of cyberbullying can include loneliness, humiliation, insecurity, and fearfulness, as well as anger, loss of self-esteem, and self-pity. Boys are more apt to experience anger, while girls tend to experience self-pity. Long-term effects can include trouble making friends, difficulty adjusting emotionally and socially, and poor relationship skills.

Unfortunately, being victimized and not dealing with one's emotions can lead to even more serious issues. Victims are more likely to engage in delinquent or self-destructive behavior. Some studies point to a strong link between criminal victimization and criminal offenses, meaning as one increases, so does the other. The link is relevant, particularly for violent behaviors.

On the most serious end of the spectrum, school shootings have been linked to bullying or peer harassment. As related by Patchin and Hinduja, the United States Secret Service found that 71 percent of attackers in school-shooting incidents between 1974 and 2000 "felt bullied, persecuted, or injured by others prior to the attack." Cyberbullying will probably figure heavily in school violence, including mass shootings, once comprehensive statistics are available for the 2000s and beyond.

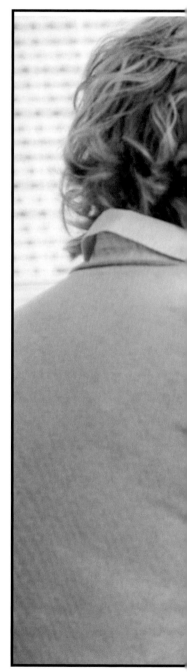

Some young people find that entering counseling or therapy is a positive step in dealing with the minor to major psychic trauma of being cyberbullied and in self-healing and recovery.

Treatments to Think About

While it may not seem like it for victims, treatment can help heal the emotional wounds of cyberbullying. With the right help and treatment plan, many young people have moved on from the negative aftermath of their harassment and gone on to lead perfectly normal lives, even thrive.

One type of treatment is called transactional analysis. The idea behind this type of therapy is that people still hold onto feelings of fear or anxiety from the past. These feelings can then affect a person in the future, so the therapy focuses on the connection between the past and current issues. For bullying targets, they may have lingering issues from when they were harassed or abused by a bully.

Another type of treatment is called assertiveness training. Cyberbullying can affect the victim's self-confidence. Assertiveness training addresses this directly by teaching people the proper techniques for standing up to bullies. In doing so, it is hoped that their confidence is restored. They may also begin standing up for themselves in other interactions with people, which will help their self-confidence and success in relationships, school, and work, too.

Cognitive behavioral therapy, or CBT, is another option. Cyberbullying can change a young person's behavior and thoughts, as he or she adapts in order to deal with the depression or anxiety resulting from the stressful situation. CBT retrains a person to overcome these behaviors to make a positive change in ongoing daily life.

CBT has been shown to be one of the most effective ways to address the emotional stress caused by bullying and is widely used. It teaches young people to understand their thoughts and feelings, as well as how they can influence their actions and behavior. Often young people are not aware that they are engaging in self-destructive behavior that is indirectly caused by bullying. CBT aims to replace negative coping mechanisms with positive ones to improve self-worth and confidence. Many of the benefits of CBT include improved communication with others, the ability to deal with fears, stepping

Coming Back from Despair: Ally Del Monte

Ally Del Monte refused to give in when she was pushed to extreme measures by her cyberbullies. While in the eighth grade, thirteen-year-old Ally attempted suicide after years of bullying, including 272 Tumblr messages telling her to kill herself. She

(continued on the next page)

(continued from the previous page)

kept it all a secret, hoping things would get better. But after her mother intervened, things got better, according to a story about her ordeal and recovery in USA Today.

As a tenth grader, Ally shared her story and posted a video on her blog, LoserGurl.com. She received positive responses from kids around the world who thanked her for helping them through their own situations. Part of her recovery process has been to use social media to spread a positive message. She said that she has talked many people out of committing suicide and started an antibullying campaign called #bebrave. She told USA Today, "By sharing my story, I hope I can show kids that it does get better."

back from destructive thoughts, and improved self-esteem.

Treating the Bully

While many recovery strategies focus on the victim, cyberbullies can also get help. According to *Psychology Today*, research has highlighted several of the serious consequences cyberbullies face, including suicide,

Cyberbullies have their own issues that they must address to avoid long-term effects such as academic problems, substance abuse, and suicide. Many have deep-seated insecurities.

academic problems, substance abuse, and mental health problems. It is important to remember that these bullies are often just kids themselves.

Bullies commonly misdirect their anger, projecting their pain as a result of abuse from another bully or an abusive family member. One type of treatment bullies can undergo is anger management.

Bullies can learn how to properly express their anger while also learning relaxation techniques. Similarly, psychotherapy can get to the root of why their anger is being misdirected in the first place. This type of therapy is commonly known as talk therapy.

One relatively effective method is to have an intervention with the bully. It is a good way to communicate the damage the bully's behavior is causing. Interventions are usually conducted with the bully's family and sometimes the victims themselves.

Counselors can speak to the bully one-on-one, in order to understand his or her situation and background. The bully can also practice introspection with a counselor and learn how his or her actions can affect others in significant ways. Bullies need to feel cared for just like anyone else, and they can also develop empathy for others. It is important that the bully not feel threatened during treatment or else the bully can become unwilling to work toward positive change.

The American Counseling Association Program

The American Counseling Association, or ACA, developed a program to help victims move on and recover from cyberbullying incidents. The ACA, the world's largest association representing professional counselors, aimed to involve families in the recovery process. They also integrated technology into their program, hoping to counter any negative associations victims may develop toward the technologies used to harass them. The ACA hopes that this short-term strategy will result in cyberbullying victims being able to thrive and use the same tools their peers do, if they so desire, in the long run.

Advanced technology has been in use for therapeutic purposes for years, such as virtual reality exposure therapy gaming, used since 2005, and online cinematherapy since 2008. However, counseling for cyberbullying is still in its infancy, a trend the ACA hopes to change with its recommendation of using these technologies, as well as video games, Facebook, and YouTube.

An Ongoing Recovery

The recovery process is not always a straightforward process and is usually not a speedy one, either. It can take time. Many programs, such as the ACA's, can take weeks or months. Therapy sessions can require multiple visits to uncover deep-seated issues. Cognitive behavioral therapy can also take time to allow positive behaviors to replace negative ones. Victims in recovery should remain focused on the recovery and not become frustrated when the process possibly takes longer than initially assumed. Luckily, counseling and support groups can shepherd a young person through the dark days. Either in person or online, there are numerous options out there.

If you have been cyberbullied, you may naturally continue to feel unsafe on your old favorite electronic stomping grounds, such as Instagram, Facebook, or other sites. Rules such as when technology can be used may need to be changed as the situation evolves. Perhaps a victim's recovery is showing progress and he or she may not need as many therapy sessions. Each situation and each student is different, and recovery will be, too. Prevention strategies also take time to implement and should be given a fair amount of time to be successful.

Hopeful Trends

More recent studies have shown a reduction in cyberbullying numbers. According to *US News & World Report*, the School Crime Supplement to the 2013 National Crime Victimization Survey showed that bullying in general had declined. At 6.9 percent in 2013, fewer students reported being cyberbullied than the 9 percent in 2011. Former US Education Secretary Arne Duncan stated that although there much progress has been made in this area, more improvements could be made.

Other research shows that most cyberbullying incidents are now minor, with serious incidents less common. David Finkelhor, director of the Crimes Against Children Research Center, agreed that the frequency of cyberbullying incidents has been reduced over the last ten years.

Moving Forward

One of the reaction strategies discussed by many professionals is to disengage from abusive friends or groups by blocking or unfriending them on social media. More extreme responses are withdrawing entirely from social contact, except for the bare minimum of going to classes and being outside on the way to and from school or errands.

There are many activities victims can engage in on their own. Many people have experienced the positive aspects of solo physical fitness routines such as weightlifting, yoga, or jogging. Other ways to unwind and gain strength again include faith-based pursuits, such as prayer and church, temple, or mosque services. Taking some time to catch up on reading for fun or pleasure, or to learn new things, is a good way to clear one's head, too.

It is not healthy to remain alone forever. Humans are social animals who depend on interactions with

Enjoying quality time with cherished friends can definitely help one recover from the trauma of bullying.

others like them, and this is true even for self-professed loners. For victims, moving on from their situation may require reaching out to a new social circle, particularly in cases where friends are the cyberbullies. New friends can be made in a therapeutic setting or while enjoying a new hobby or activity such as afterschool jobs, sports, or clubs. Extracurricular activities could connect you with some positive people who are interested in things you like and who will get to know and appreciate you for who you are. Volunteering, charity work, and activism are other options. These worlds tend to attract sympathetic, helpful, and kind people. There are even many antibullying initiatives that young people can take part in, whether at their school or within their community.

Part of the recovery process is learning who is a true friend and who is not. There are many options for young people to get reintegrated into the real world. If you have suffered cyberbullying, hopefully you can bounce back quickly. There is a whole world waiting out there, once you take the necessary steps.

Glossary

anonymous Not named or identified, or hiding one's identity.

callousness Feeling or showing no sympathy for others.

cinematherapy A form of therapy involving the viewing of thought-provoking or inspiring films.

cyberbullying The use of electronic communications to bully, intimidate, threaten, or denigrate a person, including ruining his or her reputation.

cyberstalking The use of technology to pursue a person obsessively, and harass them.

deliberate Describes something that is done or said on purpose.

delinquent Offending by neglect or violation of duty or of law.

denigration To criticize unfairly or harshly diminish.

empathy An awareness of and ability to share another person's feelings, especially if the person is somehow in pain.

exacerbate To make a problem or bad situation worse.

exclusion Keeping or shutting someone out of a group or activity.

flaming To send a hostile or rude electronic message to someone or about someone.

harassment Bothering or pressuring someone constantly and aggressively.

impersonation To pretend to be some other person.

mob mentality When multiple people are influenced by their peers to adopt certain behaviors or follow trends.

perception A mental impression or understanding of something.

plight A difficult or dangerous situation.

predictor An early symptom or indication of an issue or problem.

punitive Intended to inflict punishment for a crime or breaking a rule.

retaliate To return in kind, as an injury, or get revenge.

withdrawn Describes someone who tends to avoid interaction or communication with other people.

For More Information

Family Acceptance Project
1600 Holloway Avenue
San Francisco, CA 94132
Email: fap@sfsu.edu
Website: https://familyproject.sfsu.edu

The Family Acceptance Project focuses on the needs of the LGBT youth community by preventing health and mental health risks within families and communities. They provide training and resources for families across the country.

Kids Help Phone
300-439 University Avenue
Toronto, ON M5G 1Y8
Canada
(416) 586-5437
Website: http://www.kidshelpphone.ca

As Canada's only toll-free, twenty-four-hour phone and web counseling service, Kids Help Phone is an anonymous service that also provides helpful resources and information for those in need.

Megan Meier Foundation
515 Jefferson, Suite A
St. Charles, MO 63301

(636) 757-3501

Email: info@meganmeierfoundation.org

Website: http://www.meganmeierfoundation.org

Founded in 2007 by the mother of a cyberbullying victim, the Megan Meier Foundation is a global bullying and cyberbullying prevention foundation. The organization holds numerous events and leads several programs aimed to end cyberbullying and suicide.

PACER's National Bullying Prevention Center

8161 Normandale Boulevard

Bloomington, MN 55437

Email: Bullying411@PACER.org

Website: http://www.pacer.org/bullying

PACER's National Bullying Prevention Center's goal is to end bullying by providing resources for students, parents, teachers, and more. Their collection of websites are targeted to different age groups and provide ways for teens to have their voices heard.

PREVNet

Queen's University

98 Barrie Street

Kingston, ON K7L 3N6

Canada

(613) 533-2632

Website: http://www.prevnet.ca

PREVNet, or Promoting Relationships and Eliminating Violence Network, is a network of Canadian research scientists and youth-oriented organizations with the common goal of stopping bullying and promoting safe and healthy relationships.

STOMP Out Bullying!

220 East 57th Street

New York, NY 10022

Website: http://www.stompoutbullying.org

Created in 2005, STOMP Out Bullying! is a national leader in bullying and cyberbullying prevention for young people.

Websites

Because of the changing nature of internet links, Rosen Publishing has developed an online list of websites related to the subject of this book. This site is updated regularly. Please use this link to access the list:

http://www.rosenlinks.com/COP/cyberbully

For Further Reading

Bauman, Sheri, Donna Cross, and Jenny L. Walker. *Principles of Cyberbullying Research: Definitions, Measures, and Methodology*. New York, NY: Routledge, 2013.

Breguet, Teri. *Frequently Asked Questions About Cyberbullying*. New York, NY: The Rosen Publishing Group, 2007.

Brown, Tracy. *Cyberbullying: Online Safety*. New York, NY: Rosen Publishing, 2014.

Gerdes, Louise I. *Cyberbullying*. Detroit, MI: Greenhaven Press, 2012.

Head, Honor. *How to Handle Cyberbullying*. Mankato, MN: Smart Apple Media, 2015.

Katz, Farley. *Journal of a Schoolyard Bully: Cyberbully*. New York, NY: St. Martin's Griffin, 2012.

McGarry, Katie. *Walk the Edge*. Don Mills, ON, Canada: Harlequin Teen, 2016.

Nelson, Drew. *Dealing with Cyberbullies*. New York, NY: Gareth Stevens Pub., 2013.

Neville, Ann. *R.I.P. Cyberbullying: A Guide for Parents*. Hamilton, New Zealand: CreateBooks New Zealand, 2014.

Patchin, Justin W., and Sameer Hinduja. *Words Wound: Delete Cyberbullying and Make Kindness Go Viral*. Minneapolis, MN: Free Spirit Pub, 2013.

Spivet, Bonnie. *Stopping Cyberbullying*. New York, NY: PowerKids Press, 2012.

Bibliography

Bidwell, Allie. "School Bullying, Cyberbullying Continue to Drop." *U.S. News & World Report*, March 15, 2015. http://www.usnews.com/news /blogs/data-mine/2015/05/15/school-bullying -cyber-bullying-continue-to-drop.

"Cyberpsychologist Mary Aiken on Protecting Teenagers from Cyberbullies." CBS News, August 23, 2016. http://www.cbsnews.com /news/cyberbullying-prevention-social-media -teenagers-mary-aiken-cyberpsychologist.

Demaray, Michelle Kilpatrick. "Why Do Some Kids Cyberbully Others?" *Psychology Today*, April 26, 2013. https://www.psychologytoday.com/blog /the-wide-wide-world-psychology/201304 /why-do-some-kids-cyberbully-others.

Dempsey, Ernest. *Recovering the Self: A Journal of Hope and Healing*. Ann Arbor, MI: Loving Healing Press, 2010.

Elliot, Michele. *Bullies, Cyberbullies and Frenemies*. London, UK: Wayland, 2013.

Grider, Olivia. "Public Relations Students Empower Kids to Stand Strong against Bullying." CESR, June 18, 2014. http://cesr.ua.edu/public -relations-students-empower-kids-to-stand -strong-against-bullying.

Hinduja, Sameer, and Justin W. Patchin. "Cyberbullying Warning Signs." Cyberbullying

Research Center, October 24, 2014. http://cyberbullying.org/cyberbullying-warning-signs.

Hinduja, Sameer, and Justin W. Patchin. *School Climate 2.0: Preventing Cyberbullying and Sexting One Classroom at a Time.* Thousand Oaks, CA: Corwin Press, 2012.

Holmes, Linda. "'The Bully Project' Finds Its Moment." NPR, June 23, 2011. http://www.npr.org/sections/monkeysee/2011/06/23/137362129/the-bully-project-finds-its-moment.

Leefeldt, Ed. "Victim of Cyberbullying? Insurance Might Help." CBS News, May 10, 2016. http://www.cbsnews.com/news/victim-of-cyberbullying-insurance-might-help.

Lenhart, Amanda. "Teens, Social Media & Technology Overview 2015." Pew Research Center, April 09, 2015. http://www.pewinternet.org/2015/04/09/teens-social-media-technology-2015/.

Lohmann, Raychelle Cassada. "Teen Bullying: A CBT Approach to Addressing the Issue." *Psychology Today*, June 27, 2013. https://www.psychologytoday.com/blog/teen-angst/201306/teen-bullying-cbt-approach-addressing-the-issue.

Magid, Larry. "Preventing And Recovering from Bullying—What Works And What Doesn't." *Forbes*, November 12, 2013. http://www.forbes.com/sites/larrymagid/2013/11/12/preventing-and-recovering-from-bullying-what-works-and-what-doesnt.

Mendoza, Jessica. "Technology Gave Rise to Cyberbullying. Can It Also Stop It?" *Christian Science Monitor*, April 22, 2015. http://www.csmonitor.com/Technology/2015/0422/Technology-gave-rise-to-cyberbullying.-Can-it-also-stop-it.

Olsen, Jane. "Responding to Cyberbullying in Safe and Constructive Ways." MSU Extension, February 20, 2012. http://msue.anr.msu.edu/news/responding_to_cyberbullying_in_safe_and_constructive_ways.

Patchin, Justin W., and Sameer Hinduja. *Cyberbullying Prevention and Response: Expert Perspectives*. New York, NY: Routledge, 2012.

Psych Central News editor. "Cyberbullying Rampant for Lesbian and Gay Teens." Live Science, March 10, 2010. http://www.livescience.com/6199-cyberbullying-rampant-lesbian-gay-teens.html.

Suhay, Lisa. "Calgary Bullied Teen's Loving Response Earns Her Love in Return." *Christian*

Science Monitor, October 16, 2014. http://www
.csmonitor.com/The-Culture/Family/Modern
-Parenthood/2014/1016/Calgary-bullied
-teens-loving-response-earns-her-love-in
-return.

Swearer, Susan M., Dorothy L. Espelage, and Scott A. Napolitano. *Bullying Prevention and Intervention: Realistic Strategies for Schools.* New York, NY: Guilford Press, 2009.

White, Gerald J. *Cyber Bullying—Myths and Facts: Some Findings from Research in Newfoundland and Labrador Schools.* Newfoundland and Labrador, Canada: Newfoundland and Labrador Centre for Applied Health Research, 2015.

Index

About the Author

Jeff Mapua is the author of several books on technology, including *Making the Most of Crowdfunding* and *A Career in Customer Service and Tech Support*. He also has written about modern issues, including *a* biography of transgender activist Lana Wachowski. Jeff lives in Dallas, Texas, with his wife, Ruby.

Photo Credits

Cover pp. 6-7 Highwaystarz-Photography/iStock/Thinkstock; p. 9 Yalana/iStock/Thinkstock; pp. 10-11, 74-75 oneinchpunch/iStock/Thinkstock; pp. 14-15, 41 monkeybusinessimages/iStock/Thinkstock; pp. 18-19 michaeljung/iStock/Thinkstock; pp. 23, 60-61 DGLimages/iStock/Thinkstock; pp. 24-25 © iStockphoto.com/asiseeit; pp. 28-29 mrohana/iStock/Thinkstock; pp. 30-31 stock-eye/iStock/Thinkstock; p. 33 lorenzoantonucci/iStock/Thinkstock; pp. 44-45 omgimages/iStock/Thinkstock; p. 49 Wavebreakmedia Ltd/Wavebreak Media/Thinkstock; pp. 50-51 Paul/Thinkstock; p. 53 SpeedKingz/Shutterstock.com; p. 57 michaelpuche/iStock/Thinkstock; pp. 64-65 OcusFocus/iStock/Thinkstock; p. 66 Ryan McVay/Photodisc/Thinkstock; pp. 72-73 Monkey Business Images/Monkey Business/Thinkstock; pp. 78-79 Jupiterimages/Creatas/Thinkstock; p. 81 NicolasMcComber/E+/Getty Images; p. 85 Purestock/Thinkstock; pp. 86-87 AlexRaths/iStock/Thinkstock; p. 91 dobok/iStock/Thinkstock; pp. 96-97 BananaStock/Thinkstock; cover and interior pages background © iStockphoto.com/Sergei Dubrovski.

Designer: Nicole Russo-Duca; Photo Researcher: Philip Wolny